learn to SPEAK MUSIC

WRITTEN BY
JOHN CROSSINGHAM

DESIGN & ILLUSTRATIONS BY
JEFF KULAK

Owlkids Books Inc.
10 Lower Spadina Avenue, Suite 400, Toronto, Ontario M5V 2Z2
www.owlkids.com

Parents and Guardians: Please use your own discretion when deciding if the songs in the playlists are appropriate for your children.

Distributed in Canada by Raincoast Books
9050 Shaughnessy Street, Vancouver, British Columbia V6P 6E5

Distributed in the United States by Publishers Group West
1700 Fourth Street, Berkeley, California 94710

Special thanks to Michael Bellissimo, Mike Byj, Eva Kwok, Daniel Longmire, Nick Zubeck, and the OWL Think Tank.

Library and Archives Canada Cataloguing in Publication

Crossingham, John, 1974-
      Learn to speak music : a guide to creating, performing, and promoting your songs / John Crossingham ; illustrated by Jeff Kulak.

Includes index.
ISBN 978-1-897349-64-9 (bound).--ISBN 978-1-897349-65-6 (pbk.)

      1. Popular music--Vocational guidance--Juvenile literature.

2. Popular music--Writing and publishing--Juvenile literature.

I. Kulak, Jeff, 1983- II. Title.

ML3795.C76 2009   j782.42'164023   C2009-901004-6

Library of Congress Control Number: 2009923331

Design and illustration: Jeff Kulak

Canada Council   Conseil des Arts
for the Arts   du Canada

ONTARIO ARTS COUNCIL
CONSEIL DES ARTS DE L'ONTARIO

We acknowledge the financial support of the Canada Council for the Arts, the Ontario Arts Council, the Government of Canada through the Book Publishing Industry Development Program (BPIDP), and the Government of Ontario through the Ontario Media Development Corporation's Book Initiative for our publishing activities.

Printed in China

A   B   C   D   E   F

Publisher of Chirp, chickaDEE and OWL
www.owlkids.com

For my girls—J.C.

For my grandparents—J.K.

LEARN TO SPEAK MUSIC

SPEAK UP!

Have you ever heard people call music "the universal language" and wondered what they meant by that? After all, you've never heard anyone actually "speak" music, right? That's just silly...

OK, true, no one actually *speaks* music. Not like how people speak English, or French, or German, or Spanish. But it is something that everyone around the world understands, even if they can't talk to each other.

That's why Russian music like Tchaikovsky's Nutcracker Suite gets played every holiday season in North America. Or how pop acts like The Killers or Beyoncé can sell out huge concerts in Japan—even though all the words are in English!

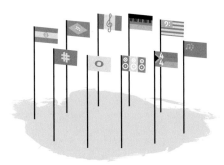

You see, we use language to tell each other things like "I'm hungry," or "Let's go outside and play." Music does that too—it's just the message is a little different. Some music says, "I'm sad," or "I miss you." Other music says, "I'm happy," or "Let's dance!" But all music around the world says *something*.

Of course, most of us don't look at music like that. It's just really fun to listen to and to play. And you're surrounded by so much of it—at school, at the mall, with friends, on TV—that the world can seem a little overcrowded by songs. But there's always room for one more song, one more voice.

That's what learning to *speak* music is all about—finding a way to tell other people your most fun, special, sad, crazy, silly stories. Through music!

So just who am I to talk about this stuff anyway? Hey, good question!

Hi, I'm John, and I'm a musician and the author of this book. I've put out seven albums and toured the world a bunch of times with different bands—the biggest one being indie band Broken Social Scene. You might've even seen me play with them on TV a couple of times. But the most important thing about me is this: I'm not the world's greatest singer, guitarist, or drummer. Heck, I only started playing music when I was about twelve or thirteen—maybe around the age you are right now. And yet, I got to do the very things I always dreamed I could. The one thing that always saw me through wasn't tons of talent, it was just a love of music. You get where I'm going with this? If I can do it…Exactly, so can you.

CHAPTER 1

Making Music

You're dancing in your room, listening to your favorite band. Again.
In fact, you've just listened to that one song four times in a row!
"This song is so awesome! How do they do it?!"

Well, how *did* they do it? How did they take all those little notes and cram them together to make such an awesome tune? They must be geniuses...Totally, they ARE geniuses!

Sure, maybe they are, but so are *you*. And making music isn't as tough as it sounds. Here are the straight goods:

· Music isn't complex.

· Music is whatever you want it to be.

· You already know how to make music.

Now, I don't mean this in some kind of lame, feel-good sort of way. And I certainly am not trying to say that playing music doesn't require effort, study, or practice.

But none of us ever took some course that taught us how to enjoy music, or what music it was that we liked. We don't attend the school of air guitar or shower-singing either.

That's because music, and the desire to listen to it and play it, is instinctual. In each of us exists a weird little musical animal waiting to be discovered.

Speaking of animals, it's not just people who dig music—birds, whales, dolphins, monkeys, crickets, and so many other animals use their own songs to send messages back and forth to each other.

So you see, whether you collect it, listen to it, or make it, music is just something we animals do. It's in our blood.

WHY MUSIC *MATTERS*

How often have you heard someone say that music changed their life? Maybe you feel the same way, too?

It turns out that when people say that music changed them, they really mean it! That's because music is something that actually affects our minds and our bodies. There are a lot of different reasons why, but most of it comes down to two things: pitch and rhythm. We humans can't get enough of it!

 + 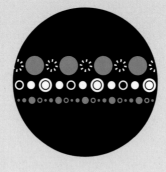 =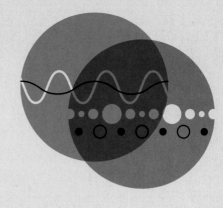

HERE'S THE PITCH...

Pitch is the way that sounds go up and down. Want an example? Get a rubber band and wrap it around your thumb and finger. Stretch it as tight as you can and pluck it with another finger. *Boing!* Now loosen the band a little and pluck again. *Bi-youm!* Sounds lower, doesn't it? That's pitch—tighter sounds are higher, while looser sounds are lower.

...AND HERE'S THE BEAT!

You might know rhythm by its more popular name—the beat. A beat is the very thing that gets toes tapping and bodies grooving. Faster beats make us feel excited. Slower beats make us feel calm.

NOW, ADD IT UP...

Music is any series of sounds that combine pitch and rhythm. As long as you combine those two things, you can use pretty much anything to create music. (So the next time your folks say it's just a bunch of noise, you tell them, "Actually, by virtue of its artistic merging of pitch and rhythm, it technically is music, Dad.")

Melody maker

A melody is series of notes played together. Pitch and rhythm work together to make a melody. Go ahead, pick a favorite melody from a song right now and sing it. Look at how it's not just the way that the sounds go up and down, but also the timing of each sound that makes the melody what it is. If you change either the pitch or rhythm of the any of the notes, the melody changes!

...AND TURN IT UP!

While we're at it, let's not forgot about volume! Soft, gentle music is soothing and romantic. But whether it's throbbing metal, pounding dance music, or even the swelling peak of a symphony, loud music is really thrilling.

DYNAMITE!

Wanna see volume in action? Everyone from punk bands to orchestras and jazz bands use dynamics in their music. Dynamics is how music moves from loud to quiet and back again.

PLAYLIST
Dynamics

In the late 1980s an underground college band called The Pixies was so good at using dynamics that they influenced tons of other bands, like Nirvana, to do the same in their songs. Check out how these tunes hit you hard!

THE PIXIES » "GIGANTIC"

This one starts small with a simple bassline and some vocals before it gets, well, gigantic.

BEETHOVEN » "FIFTH SYMPHONY, FIRST MOVEMENT"

"Bah-bah-bah Bahm!" Everyone knows this intro, but listen beyond it to hear how smoothly the music rises and falls—classical music is some of the most dynamic stuff around.

KELLY CLARKSON » "SINCE U BEEN GONE"

The verse is quieter on purpose to make this stunning chorus as explosive as possible. *Ka-boom!*

CHOOSING *an* INSTRUMENT

There are many different instruments that you can use to express yourself.

It's the first step as a budding young musician—finding the instrument or style that best suits you. This isn't a permanent choice, and you can learn to play lots of instruments. But to begin, you should try to find one that speaks to you. That's right— it turns out that an instrument has a voice all its own.

TIMBER, ER, I MEAN, *TIMBRE!*

An instrument's voice is called its timbre. You can think of it as the difference between the way your speaking voice sounds and someone else's. Trumpets, violins, guitars, and saxophones can all play many of the same notes—it's the particular type of sound each of them makes that's unique. Is there an instrument whose timbre really moves you?

THE PRICE TAG

Of course, no instrument is going to move you if you can't take it home. The price is a big deal. Guitars are fairly cheap—you can find a decent starter guitar for a couple hundred dollars—but drums and keyboards can be a lot more. Many schools and music schools have instruments that you can use while you're saving up.

A USED-FUL OPTION

Second-hand instruments are a beginner's best friend. Go to different music stores and examine their stuff. Before buying, consider the following:

· Is the store in good shape? How about the instruments?

· Has the instrument been repaired in the past? What needed to be fixed before it was ready to sell?

· Does it have a warranty? If so, how long is the instrument protected for?

· Is the brand of instrument reliable?

Before you go, do some research and read some reviews of different brands. Bring a musician friend or adult to the store to help you choose. If you're smart (and a little lucky), that cheap little instrument can last your whole life.

BUYING A GUITAR

It's no secret that most budding musicians begin by learning guitar —it's portable, fairly cheap, and easy to learn. But what to buy?

The most well-known guitars are Gibsons and Fenders, and they don't come cheap. You could easily pay over a thousand dollars for one! Thankfully, both manufacturers have discount brands—Gibson's is called Epiphone and Fender's is called Squier. In addition, there are dozens of knock-off brands that offer look-alikes for even cheaper. But buyer beware: the craftsmanship can be a bit weak. Be sure to test out the instrument first.

Popular or unique?

A guitar sure looks cool, but when everyone plays one, it's tough to stand out. Why not consider learning the drums or a horn instead? Not only are these instruments awesome in their own way, but you'll be that much more attractive as a future band member.

Look Sharp!

Looks are not the only reason to buy an instrument, but the more you and a guitar look great together, the more you'll want to be together.

66 When you buy a guitar, strap it on and check yourself out in the mirror. Does it look wicked? Good. You'll need all the motivation you can muster to keep practicing! 99

—Andrew Whiteman
LEAD GUITARIST, BROKEN SOCIAL SCENE

Learning the Craft

Learning to play an instrument is like making a new friend—it's a little awkward at first. But just like that new friend, it can be really good to you if you stick with it. Fortunately, there are ways to help you do this.

PREACH ON, TEACHER!

Whether you've never touched an instrument or you're a total hotshot, music lessons can really help. Lessons are about more than learning the basics. A great teacher keeps you challenged as your skills improve. Lessons cost money, so expect a lot from your teacher—and yourself. Before you sign up, tell the teacher what you hope to learn. It's important that you're both working toward the same goals. Once you're agreed, keep up your end by showing up on time for lessons and following the practice schedule your teacher gives you.

THE SELF-TAUGHT MUSICIAN

If lessons aren't in your budget, don't sweat it. Lots of great musicians are self-taught. If you're up to the challenge, here's how to take yourself to school:

Find a great how-to book—There are tons of instructional books out there. Many come with DVDs or CDs.

Play along with songs—Pick some favorite songs and try to figure out the parts. Learning to play by ear is a great exercise.

Talk to other musicians—If you're really stuck, seek out someone else who plays your instrument and pick their brain. Fellow musicians are the greatest resource for secret clues and hints.

It's Contagious

Sometimes a teacher's greatest gift isn't some complex lesson or magical technique. It's the simplest encouragement and a love of playing that sticks with you over the years.

66 At music school I had a great teacher named Mr. Edwards. He loved singing so much, and his passion made us all love it too. I will never forget when he said, 'You've got a pretty voice, Melissa, you just need a little more confidence.' To this day, when in doubt, I turn to his words for guidance. 99

—*Melissa Auf der Maur*
**BASSIST/SINGER, AUF DER MAUR,
(FORMERLY OF SMASHING
PUMPKINS AND HOLE)**

what
inspires
you?

OH, I'LL NEVER GET IT!

At first a lot of what you'll play on any instrument will sound nothing like the awesome stuff you hear in your head. Hey, you are only learning. The truth is, even the best musicians struggle sometimes. That's why inspiration is so important.

IT'S EVERYWHERE YOU LOOK

Inspiration is what keeps you playing, even if you're feeling down. You can find it anywhere you like, in any music you like. Pianists can be inspired by drummers. Jazz musicians can be inspired by rock stars. Punk singers can be inspired by opera greats. And most of all, passion is way more important than ability—punk, blues, hip hop, and many more genres all have big stars who were never the greatest musicians. They just believed in themselves and loved what they did.

ALWAYS LOOKING TO LEARN

John Coltrane was one of the all-time greatest saxophone players who ever lived. He could play any style, from tender ballads to fiery live songs that lasted an hour! But most impressive was how humble and dedicated he was. Coltrane was always looking to learn. He practiced for hours every day. Even when he was considered the best sax man in jazz, he still asked other players for tips.

PLAY BECAUSE YOU LOVE IT

Watching friends make amazing albums can really inspire you to do the best you can with your own albums and performances. And the dedication of other musicians is pretty inspiring. But the bottom line is that no one gets anywhere in music if they aren't enjoying themselves. If you find yourself getting frustrated with your instrument, take a break. If you and that instrument were meant to betogether, you'll find your way back to it eventually.

PLAYLIST
Inspiration

When an artist is truly inspired to create, his or her music really shines, and that inspires others, too.

JOHN COLTRANE » "A LOVE SUPREME"
Coltrane wrote this four-piece suite as a deeply personal dedication to God.

JEFF BUCKLEY » "HALLELUJAH"
Buckley liked to call himself a chanteuse— a French term for a female singer! His delicate, falsetto style has inspired everyone from Radiohead's Thom Yorke to Chris Martin of Coldplay.

MISSY ELLIOT » "GET UR FREAK ON" (CLEAN)
This track took its rhythms from classical Indian tabla drumming. Producer Timbaland draws inspiration for this and other hip hop and R&B songs from around the world.

CHAPTER 2

Form a Band

As soon as you begin feeling comfortable with an instrument, chances are you'll want to form a band. After all, that's what everyone does…*right?*

Well, why *do* people form bands? Many musicians enjoy the complete freedom of playing alone—no one to answer to, no one to argue with. Truth is, playing solo *can* be very rewarding. But as the saying goes, "With great freedom comes great responsibility." In other words, if you screw up, you're on your own!

Maybe we form bands for the same reasons that we make friends—some experiences are both more fun and easier when you can share them with others. Not only do bandmates give you someone to wink at knowingly when everything is clicking, but more people means more variety of instruments, more ideas, more volume, just MORE!

Like with any group of friends, keeping a band together takes work. You have to listen to each other. You have to respect that not everyone wants to do the same thing as you. But it is worth the effort. Playing music in a band boosts your confidence if you're a little shy, helps you learn faster, and is as much fun as anything you could do.

BUILDING *the* BEAST

To put it simply, a band is a group of musicians who play music together. The most traditional lineup is guitar/bass/drums/singer. This model is affordable, and the instruments are easy to learn. You can play almost anything this way—punk, pop, metal, country.

And this lineup covers rhythm, chords, and melodies well. To understand what different instruments bring to a band, it helps to imagine it as an animal. Think of it as the way the drums, bass, guitar, vocals, and other instruments come together to form a musical beast.

THE SKELETON

This is the rhythm section, which is usually the drummer and the bassist. Like a real skeleton, the rhythm section—especially the drummer—supports everything else in the band.

Skeleton instruments: drums, bass, drum machine, shakers, tambourines

THE MUSCLES AND TISSUE

These are the instruments that play chords. Chords are groups of notes that are laid over the rhythm—like meat on the bones. With the rhythm and the chords, you pretty much have your finished animal. It's just a little…naked.

Muscle instruments: keyboards, guitar, piano

THE SKIN, FUR, AND FEATHERS

It's time for the melodies, which come from the singer and sometimes the guitarist. Like an animal's stripes or markings, the melodies are often the most recognizable thing about your band's music.

Furry instruments: vocals, horns, strings, lead guitar, keyboards, piano

FRANKENSTEIN'S BAND!

Once you get the hang of it, this whole animal idea makes a lot of sense. Many metal and hard rock bands have more than one guitarist, to add extra "muscle" to their band. Pop bands can use strings and horns to give their animal extra flair, like the proud feathers of a peacock. So if you're wondering how to form the band of your dreams, try asking yourself this: What animal would it be?

PLAYLIST
Who's In?

If you have a friend who plays saxophone, another who's a violinist, and you play guitars, then you've got a band. Here are some bands who also said, "Why can't we be a band?"

THE WHITE STRIPES » "BLACK MATH"

Duos like the White Stripes make a powerful, urgent racket with nothing more than guitar, vocals, and drums most of the time.

ARCADE FIRE » "WAKE UP"

On the other hand, huge bands like Arcade Fire take the stage with a small army of instruments (and other oddities!) to create a truly massive sound.

THE ROOTS FEATURING NELLY FURTADO » "SACRIFICE"

In a world dominated by drum machines and DJs, this awesome Philadelphia group sets itself apart by being a live hip hop band.

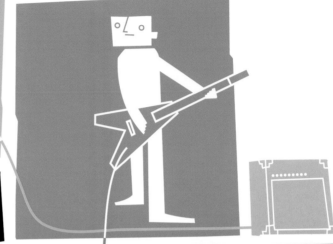

COME
TOGETHER

Anyone who wants to form a band has probably dreamt of what type of band that might be—how you'll dress, what you'll sound like, that sort of thing. But let's not get ahead of ourselves. You still need some other living, breathing humans to play with you!

There's no end to the different ways that bands can come together—chance meetings, lifelong friendships, even bitter enemies have evolved to form terrific bands. And as much as you're looking for someone, others may be looking for you, too.

FINDING MEMBERS

One of the oldest ways to find band members is still one of the best ways. That's right, a simple photocopied poster put up around your school, library, local café, or record store speaks volumes. You can also make an electronic version to circulate by email or post on your website. Be sure to include the following information:

Which instrument you play and the types of musicians you're looking for:

A list of your favorite musicians/bands (aka your influences):

If this all sounds a little too "by the book," why not be more inventive:

GUITARIST SEEKS DRUMMER AND BASSIST

SINGER NEEDED!
DO YOU DIG STEVIE WONDER, AL GREEN, & SAM COOKE? LET'S TALK!

★ ★ ★
THREE GIRLS LOOKING FOR A DRUMMER TO HELP PROVE THAT TIME TRAVEL IS POSSIBLE!
★ ★ ★

Provide an email address so people can contact you.

Tip: For safety reasons and to protect your privacy, don't use your regular email address. Instead, create a special account for recruiting band members, such as johnscoolnewband@internetmail.com. Arrange to meet the people who answer your ad at home with your parents.

Naming your band

If you think about it, a lot of band names are pretty silly: Def Leppard, Foo Fighters, Linkin Park. But they stick with you, right? The secret to a good band name is choosing one that people will remember.

If you're hard up for ideas, try brainstorming a long list of words you find interesting. They might include a scientific word (say, "electric"), or maybe a favorite animal (a fox, perhaps?) or place (skatepark). Now see what happens when you mash them. Midnight Foxes, anyone? Electric Skatepark?

The Name Game

Anything goes when coming up with a band name. Street names, strange food ingredients, foreign languages—just open your ears and go with your gut!

❝When deciding on a band name, go with instinct—if it feels and sounds right to you even after a couple of months, then it's a sticker. We liked our band name so much we even adopted it as our honorary surname.❞

—*Ellen Campesinos*
BASSIST, LOS CAMPESINOS!

23

FINDING A
SPACE

Bands are loud. *Like, really loud.*

So you need a place where you can practice without driving other people crazy. In this case, there's no place like home. It's secure, you can leave your equipment there, and it's free! But not so fast! Chances are, you'll need to convince your parents that this is a good idea. To do so, it helps to have a plan to make things as comfortable as possible for everyone.

The first thing to do is choose the best room for the job. This is almost always the basement—it's underground, which helps trap the sound, and it's out of the way. Soundproofing can get expensive, but there are some super-cheap ways around this:

· Hang old blankets on the walls—the thicker the better. This absorbs sound and stops it from bouncing around the room.

· Be kind to your neighbors and cover the windows with pillows.

· Remember to cover cracks around doors and windows while you're at it.

TIMING IS EVERYTHING

Always try to schedule practices for times that are convenient for your family. So if your parents go out polka dancing on Thursday nights, then that's when the band comes over. Go around to your neighbors' and tell them what you're up to—they'll find out anyway, and they'll be a lot more understanding and supportive of your music if you warn them first.

IS THIS THING ON?

Now that you've cut down the volume outside, it's time to turn it up inside! A public address system, or PA, is a set of microphones and speakers that amplifies (increases the volume of) a singer's voice so it can be heard over the sound of the instruments. Unfortunately, PAs aren't cheap. Stick with a very basic microphone, or mic, for vocals, and look for cheaper second-hand options at music shops and pawn stores.

SHHHHH!!!

For some people, the only good music is loud music. But there are also so many reasons *not* to play your instrument at top volume:

· It's considerate of your family and neighbors

· It teaches you to listen clearly to each other when you play

· If you have acoustic instruments like horns, they can play naturally loud without a mic (now you don't need a PA!)

· It's better for your hearing!

While we're on that, let's talk earplugs. In thirty years, you'll be glad you protected your ears during band practice. You can get a dozen earplugs for a few bucks at your local drugstore. (Don't worry, you'll get used to how they make things sound a bit muffled.) Down the road, you can even invest in professional earplugs that are molded to your ear!

Can't play at home?

So no one wants you playing at their house? Bummer. I'm sure it has nothing to do with your songs! Fortunately, there are other options out there...

· Many schools have a band room that you might be able to use after classes.

· Many cities and towns have practice spaces that are available for rent by the hour. These can get expensive, but they're useful in a pinch. You're better off finding someplace permanent.

· If all else fails, change your style for a while. Practice unplugged, play drums on pillows and cushions, whatever works. It's not ideal, but it can help keep your chops up, and a little adversity never hurt anyone.

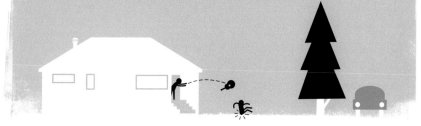

Learning a Song

You've got the band, you've got the space, now what are you going to play? The easiest way to start is to learn your favorites, the music you know best.

You've probably heard covers, where one band or musician plays another's song. Most follow the original pretty closely, but some of the more interesting ones may be better called interpretations.

Find out which songs your bandmates have been dying to try out—and begin with the easiest. Usually that means songs with fewer chords and an average beat, but you'll quickly figure out everyone's abilities.

Sometimes you can look up music and lyrics on the Internet. You'll also find guitar tabs, which are charts that help explain songs to beginners. If all else fails, listen to a song over and over and try to figure it out. Learn it slowly, one part at a time. And practice, practice, practice!

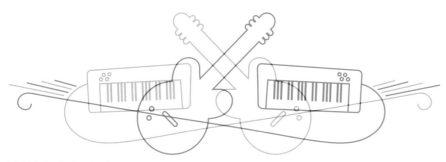

MESSING AROUND

Jamming is a slang term for playing without rules. You play a few notes or beats and see where they take you. In a jam, everyone is welcome to try stuff out—all that matters is having fun. Plus, you'll learn new things about your instrument and can introduce a musical idea that you're not quite sure about yet. Jamming can help a new band become comfortable as a group, and it lets everyone know that ideas are welcome. All right? Go jam!

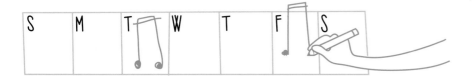

SAME TIME, SAME PLACE?

If you've got a good band you won't need to be reminded, but regular practices are a must. Practicing one or two times a week keeps everyone fresh and sharp. It's no good getting together if you've forgotten what you did the last time you practiced. Check with everyone's schedules and come up with times that work.

PLAYLIST
Take Cover!

Doing a cover of a great song can be risky—there's a lot to live up to. But pull it off, and you look like a genius! Compare these covers to their originals and see how even timeless songs can stand a change.

TALKING HEADS doing AL GREEN'S "TAKE ME TO THE RIVER"

The original is smooth soul jam. Talking Heads' singer David Byrne isn't smooth. Not at all. Instead, he uses all his nerdy, jittery charm and makes the song his own.

LUNA doing GUNS N' ROSES' "SWEET CHILD O' MINE"

The ultimate heavy metal power ballad is turned into a gentle, bedtime story of a song. Weird, but it really works.

PET SHOP BOYS doing WILLIE NELSON'S/ELVIS PRESLEY'S "ALWAYS ON MY MIND"

Neither Nelson nor Presley wrote this song, but their versions were always considered to be the classics…until this British dance-pop duo completely reinvented it.

GETTING ALONG

Even the best of friends have moments when they argue with each other. Bands are certainly no different. In fact, some bands have made it a huge part of their reputation. But if you're not interested in fighting with your guitarist every day, there are some ways around it.

COMMON GOALS

When a band first gets together and things start clicking, everything seems perfect. But then, your drummer keeps missing practice to play soccer, while your keyboardist is bugging everyone to play your first gig already. It might be time to talk about what everyone wants from this band. Do you want to:

· Play covers or original songs?

· Record some songs?

· Play a show?

It's as fun to play music as a hobby as it is to play it as a full-time job. But if half of your band wants to hang out and other half wants to tour the world, things won't last.

R-E-S-P-E-C-T

It's so simple, but respecting the ideas and abilities of your bandmates is huge. Nine out of ten band issues have something to do with people feeling left out of the band's decision-making or songwriting. How will you know how good your bassist's songs are unless you give them a try?

PICK YOUR BATTLES

People in bands can get so worked up about conflicts that they kind of fly off the handle. Hey, that's cool—people are passionate about their ideas. But you'd be surprised how many times the problem isn't as serious as it seems! Give an issue some time. If it's still bugging you a few weeks later, then talk to your band about it. Just be sure to do it in a way that doesn't accuse anyone—your bandmates might not be aware that they're doing anything to annoy you.

THE DICTATOR

Self-appointed group leaders can be annoying, but they can also get things done. Before you bail on the band, take a closer look at this person. Is your band's Napoleon just barking orders and acting tough? Or is this person really motivated—with the cool songs, strong energy, and wild ideas to back it up? While there's no need to make yourself a doormat, big personalities are sometimes the engine that really gets a band running.

THE JERK

Sometimes, you and a bandmate just don't get along. It's as simple as that. If you've really tried to patch things up, tell the band it's this person or you. Life's way too short to play in a band that makes you miserable! You'll find another band, don't worry.

CHAPTER 3

Write On!

Are you sick of being woken up to take out the garbage? Can't figure out why everyone drives cars instead of riding bikes? Is that kid in your science class ever going realize your cosmic chemistry? Or are you just unbelievably happy and wanna dance!?

These little ideas and emotions are what get us writing songs. Putting words and music together allows us to turn everyday nuggets into things people can dance and sing along to. It doesn't matter that there are already several billion songs out there. We'll always need new ones because every writer has their own personal things to say.

Being a professional songwriter and a performer is not the same thing. Some musicians just aren't cut out to write music. What's more, a band's songwriter may not be the best musician. Some musicians never write, and some writers never perform! In other words, songwriting is its very own skill, and it's one that develops slowly over time.

The best way to get an education in songwriting is by listening to other songs. As you listen, think about how they are put together. What are your favorite parts? Are there ways for you to do something similar?

⚡ POWER of SONG ⚡

It's the familiar format of pop tunes that often makes them so irresistible to our ears. Whether you're a balladeer or a punk, most of your songs will be made up of the same basic stuff—three and a half minutes of verses and choruses, with maybe a solo thrown in to spice things up. While there's no law saying you can't mix it up, part of the joy of songwriting is learning how to use each of these pieces to your song's best advantage.

The Intro

A short musical section that opens the song.

"Hello!"

The Verse

It's time for the singer to start the song's story.

"Lemme tell ya 'bout a kid from..."

The Chorus

Now the singer invites everyone to sing along—this is the catchiest part of the song.

"He was a rocket ship! Moved at a shockin' clip!"

You do the verse again.

*

Then you do the chorus again.

!

The Bridge

This is like an extra bit that songwriters like to add to spice up the song. It's a chance for the band to add a different dimension to the story.

"He's goin' around the moon…"

The Final Chorus

And end with a super-strong version of the chorus.

"Said, he's a rocket ship! A Rocking Rocket Ship!"

The Outro

A short musical section that wraps things up.

"Bye, bye!"

Many songwriters have used the format we've just shown here to put together a super-catchy song—no matter what the style of music. Here are some examples:

NEUTRAL MILK HOTEL » "HOLLAND, 1945"

RIHANNA » "UMBRELLA"

DAVID BOWIE » "CHANGES"

But tons of songs don't follow this format. Here are some that break the rules, if only a little:

THE BEATLES » "GOOD DAY SUNSHINE"
Parts of the song are in a different order. This one starts with the chorus.

RADIOHEAD » "PARANOID ANDROID"
A longer song like this one gives you the chance to explore different moods, add new parts, or tell a bigger story.

DO MAKE SAY THINK » "THE UNIVERSE!"
Songs without words are called instrumentals. In many styles of music, such as jazz, this is the most common way of writing.

33

MAKE MUSIC WORK

One of the most common questions songwriters get asked is, "What comes first: the music or the words?" Often it's the music—this is the backbone of the song. A songwriter uses music to tell the same story that the words do. That's why songs can be so powerful—your body can feel emotions and ideas at the same time as you think them in your head.

MELODIES AND PROGRESSIONS

The music in songs is generally made up of melodies and progressions.

The **melody** is usually what your vocalist sings—it's a series of single notes:

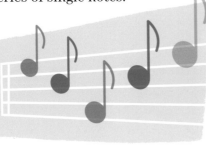

LA-LA—LA—LA—LA

A **progression** is a series of chords that are strung together:

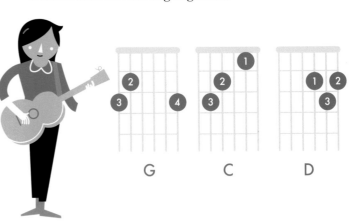

G   C   D

Progressions can be very simple. Many verses or choruses use only two or three chords.

SETTING THE SCENE

There are all sorts of choices you face as a songwriter, but few are as important as deciding on your tempo and key. These two variables set the scene for your whole song.

Tempo—This is the speed of the song. Faster songs sound more urgent, happy, angry, or excited. Slower songs can sound more thoughtful, sad, or romantic.

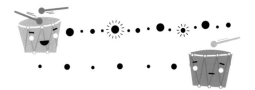

Key—You're probably aware of the two main keys used in music: major and minor. Major keys sound bright, chiming, and happy. Minor keys sound thoughtful, heavy, and sad.

IF IT FEELS RIGHT...

Now let's get something straight—few people ever sit down and say, "I'd like to write something urgent and sad, therefore I shall write a minor key in a fast tempo." Ugh, no. They just *do it*. And so will you—it's a gut reaction. But it's a good idea to understand why certain keys and tempos suggest certain moods and ideas. For example, punk bands use a lot of fast tempos because their songs are about being angry. Sugary pop songs use major keys a lot because they sound bright and happy.

Brick by Brick

Some writers create many small pieces of songs first, then later on see which of them fit together best.

66 'Mushaboom' came out pretty much complete. It was one of the songs that I've written where in twenty minutes it was done—and that doesn't often happen! Other songs, they come out in little pieces, so they just kind of lend themselves more to playing Lego with them—moving pieces around and really just keeping your ear open. 99

—*Feist*

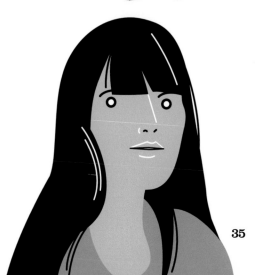

35

I've got **something** to say!

"Do you have the lyrics finished yet?" That's a question you'll hear a lot of songwriters get asked. Many singers are still working on their lyrics even as they're recording them in the studio! And for good reason too—lyrics can be tough to write.

GETTING PERSONAL

The prospect of putting your heart and soul into a song can be really intimidating. That's why the first lesson for anyone writing lyrics is to be unafraid of being bold.

If that's how you feel, then write it down. Sure, it can get a bit embarrassing, but the words are always better when they're meaningful to the person writing them. And every time you write honestly, you become better at using words to express yourself.

MUSIC: A LYRIC'S BEST FRIEND

Essentially, lyrics are poems set to music. But unlike a poem, these words don't really have to stand on their own. They work together with the music to complete the song. Many phrases that sound silly on their own can sound perfect when matched with the right music—even "ba ba ba ba-ba" can sound pretty great!

DIFFERENT STYLES

Just like music itself, lyrics come in many different styles. Remember, your lyrics can be ANYTHING you want them to be—silly, serious, true stories, made-up adventures, rants, raves, whatever!

What a character!—Many songs tell a story. Create a character (a spy? a garbage collector?) and talk about that person's day. Be sure to include lots of odd details.

You know what I really hate—Go ahead, rant about something that really bugs you. Or some*one*. Ummm, on second thought, make it something.

...but I totally love this—Or you can sing about something you really love. Or someone. No, you're right, it should be something.

Sing some gibberish—You'll be amazed how often weird phrases keep popping up. You may not know exactly what you mean by "these hazelnut bones/have me swappin' phones," but it sure is fun to sing!

RHYME IN TIME

Most lyrics are written in rhyming verse. You don't *need* to do this, but here's a good reason to—rhymes have rhythm. A good rhyming scheme goes beautifully with melody. Just like a wrong note can sound off, lines that don't rhyme often seem wrong somehow. Here are some other ways to smooth out those lines:

Switch awkward words—If a word is hard to get your tongue around, or doesn't fit well with the music, go for one that's a little easier to sing.

Cut clichés—A cliché is a phrase we've all heard a million times before, such as "I'll always love yooooou..." or "We're gonna make it!" There's nothing wrong with having the same idea, but try to find your own way to express it.

MAKE YOUR OWN SONG

Here's an exercise to help you create your very own song. You don't need to follow this exactly—few songwriters do—but it can help show just how your ideas can come together.

Just like any other recipe, you'll need some ingredients, so be sure to have:

· A guitar or piano/keyboard (these are the best songwriting instruments)

· A pen/pencil and pad of paper

· Any ideas for melodies or lyrics that you have, whether written on scraps of paper or sung into a cell phone message

Step 1

Collect all the snippets of songs you've created so far. Does anything jump out at you? Look for melodies, chord progressions, or riffs that you like.

Step 2

Play mix-and-match with these things—for example, do two melodies work well together? Or you can take a chord progression or riff and try to sing a new melody along with it. Be patient and let your mind wander a little—you're just looking for a good place to get started.

Step 3

Now that you've got a little melody and a chord progression together, it's probably going to lead to a great verse. Sing and play this part a bunch of times through until you really dig how it sounds. If you have some words scribbled down, try singing them with your new melody.

Step 4

Once your verse is feeling pretty solid, it's time to find a chorus. This is the part where you kick the song up a notch. There are all sorts of ways to do this, but here are a few to start:

Repeat, repeat, repeat—Many choruses are a simple phrase repeated over and over again.

Sing higher—Try a melody that's higher in tone than the verse. Many pop songs use this trick.

Hold that note—Some choruses also feature notes that are held for a longer time than in the verse.

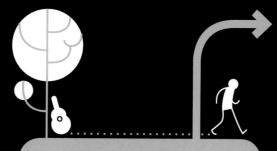

Step 6

Now is probably a good time to let it sit. Just like a cake, your song needs time to "bake." Not literally, of course, but it sometimes really helps to leave a song behind and go for a walk or something. If the song is a winner, you won't be able to get it out of your head anyway.

Step 7

How was your walk? Great! Now sit down and play the song through. Don't worry about the lyrics being finished yet or not. What do you think?

I love it! Congratulations! Polish it up and have fun playing it for friends and family!

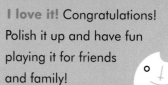

I hate it! Don't sweat it. These things happen. Just don't throw it away—you never know what new idea could turn that dud into something special!

Step 5

Play your verse and chorus back and forth and ask yourself:

Does it flow OK? The point where the chorus and verse meet is called a transition. If it feels sloppy, try adding new chords or holding a chord longer before the transition. Experiment!

Is your verse too catchy? You may find at this point that your verse sounds more like a chorus than your chorus does! Try reversing them! How is it now?

Quick tip: If you're having a bit of trouble, don't be ashamed to look to some of your favorite songs for inspiration. While it's wrong to steal something exactly, every songwriter borrows ideas from the songs they

STOP MAKING SENSE

Lots of people talk about how songs are supposed to be made. But rules are made to be broken, and that's never been truer than in songwriting. Always allow yourself the freedom to explore whatever ideas hit your eager brain. Inspiration is anywhere you can find it.

THE THESAURUS: A LYRIC'S FAVORITE DINOSAUR

OK, that thesaurus joke was lame, but not as lame as some of the rhymes out there. "You" and "blue"? "Fire" and "desire"? Too predictable! If dull rhymes are getting you down, try using a thesaurus or dictionary to spice up your vocab. Replace "you" with "emu" or "gumshoe" and see where it takes you. Sometimes an odd rhyme that you love can change an entire song for the better.

SOUNDTRACK OF YOUR LIFE

One excellent way to train your brain to embrace new musical textures is to listen carefully to movie and TV soundtracks. Anything from five-second commercial jingles to epic Oscar-winning movie scores can change your thinking. Why? Well, a soundtrack is music designed to communicate a specific mood or feeling. The best ones use unusual methods to set their scene. For example, when composer Michael Giacchino was asked to score music for the plane crash TV series *Lost*, he used broken bits from an actual plane fuselage as percussion. The result is jarring, tense, tribal music that perfectly reflects the island and its story.

BLOCK IT OUT

The sad truth about songwriting is that sometimes you'll sit down to write a song and it just doesn't happen. But what is writer's block, exactly? Often it's an indication that your brain is bored. So lay off perfecting that first draft and feed your mind something different. Maybe now is the time to listen to that new band your cousin wants you to check out. Or maybe you should read a book or help your mom and dad cook dinner. Don't be surprised if the perfect song idea hits you while you're chopping onions—hey, watch those fingers!

Tip: You never know when inspiration will strike, so never leave home without a notebook to jot down your brilliant ideas. Or what about a digital recorder? You can sing a melody into this handy recording device and then download it onto your computer later.

BRING IT TO THE BAND

Are you ready to share your songs with the rest of the band?

It's pretty cool to hear your music played for the first time, but it may not sound like you expected. So first, explain to your bandmates why you wrote the song and how you hope they'll play it. Keep in mind that even if they love every note, there's a good chance they'll want to change some things. Try not to get defensive, and really listen to their suggestions. If it doesn't seem to be working, leave it and move on to another song. Maybe now just isn't the right time for it, and that's OK. Working together, you can create something everyone is proud of.

Tip: When bandmates bring new music to the group, show you respect their efforts. You might not like the song, but they still put a lot of work into it. Make your criticism constructive, and remember to praise the parts that are working well.

COLLABORATION!

Many bands write their songs as a group. Often one member offers bits and pieces, such as a vocal melody, then everyone works together to develop the rest. Group writing is like jamming, except you're trying to capture sounds that will improve a specific idea. This method can be slow, but it really helps the band bond. Here are some good ways to approach group writing:

Hey! Do that again!—The most unexpected bend of a guitar string or run on the keyboard can trigger someone else's idea. Encourage others to explore their instruments.

What if you play that part?—Letting band members switch their parts around—such as having your keyboardist play the bassline—can change a song in unexpected but very cool ways.

Just the drums!—As the song's parts begin to add up, try using a "break." This is when only one instrument plays for a while, usually right before a verse or chorus.

Best of Both Worlds

How easy is it for a strong songwriter not to be calling all the shots? It does take some getting used to. When songwriting in a band, you'll find being a little giving can get you a lot in return.

66 When I write by myself, I don't have to answer to anybody. When I feel like that's where the bridge should go, that's where the bridge should go! But with Alexisonfire there are a lot of strong personalities in the band. It was weird at first, but now if I'm stuck on a riff, I play it for the guys and we build off it together. 99

—*Dallas Green*
SINGER/GUITARIST,
CITY AND COLOUR AND ALEXISONFIRE

CHAPTER 4

Playing Live

You always imagined it as a roar, but the crowd's actually more like a soft rumble. Voices chat to each other and chairs bump in the next room. You peek around the corner, take a deep breath, and climb on stage.

Your first time playing in front of an audience will probably be a lot like this. And even if it's just twenty people, in your gut it'll feel like the twenty thousand you've dreamed of. We all want to step on stage and blow everyone away. Come to think of it, it doesn't even matter if we know how to play an instrument—tennis rackets, table tops, and shower heads all help people live out these rock 'n' roll fantasies.

In real life, performing on stage is a few things to a musician. First off, it can be just as fun as everyone imagines—many musicians simply love being the center of attention and getting reactions from a crowd of people.

But playing live is also a real measure of a player's skills. Can you—without the trickery of the studio or the shelter of your practice space—pull off a series of songs one after another? On stage there's nowhere to hide, and let's face it, that scares most people.

So why do it at all? And if you're one of the nervous ones, does it ever get any easier? Yes, it does, but often slowly, one gig at a time.

All right then, take a deep breath and let's get you up there already!

PUT ON A SHOW

Eventually, everyone wants to put on their own show. But if you're a young band, there's one big obstacle—most music clubs are also bars, and that means no minors allowed. Or does it…?

ALL-AGES PARTY!

Well, actually, yeah it does. But don't sweat it—it's time for an all-ages show! This is exactly what it sounds like.

People of any age can come. These shows are easier to set up than you think—all it takes is a little planning. But before we get to the particulars, let's start things off with a checklist. To put on a show you need:

· A bill (lists the bands that will be playing).

· A venue (just a fancy word for location).

· A PA (if the venue doesn't already have one).

· Staff (a friend or two to help run things).

· Promotion (lets the public know about your gig).

MAKING A BILL

Before any show can happen, you need a bill. These are the bands that will play the show. You can certainly play your own show, but the more the merrier, especially when you're starting out. Other bands help share the costs, and they attract more people to the show. A bill of three to four bands often ensures a good-sized crowd.

THE HOT SPOT

A gig can happen anywhere, but some places are better than others. Check out your local cultural or community center. They may regularly host music and theater events, so they'll also have a stage and possibly a PA. Cafés, bookstores, or school auditoriums are other possibilities. Before you book a space, be sure to ask whether there's a rental fee involved.

HOME SWEET HOME?

If you have the right parents—and understanding neighbors—it's possible to have a house show. Basically, you just set the time and play for people at the same place where you practice. You may not be able to fit many people and the sound might not be great either, but none of that matters when you're starting out. It's a chance to play for people. So rock out and then order some pizza for everyone!

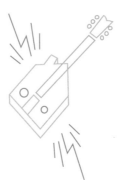

Is someone else already doing this?

Not to discourage you from setting things up yourself, but it's worth asking around to see if someone else is already putting together shows in your area—you might be able to team up and put together a really killer gig!

Open some doors

Whether you're thirteen or thirty, nearly all new bands get started as an opener—the band that goes on before the main act, or headliner. Opening slots don't just fall into your lap. You need to ask around and meet other bands to get good gigs. But stick to it and play whatever comes your way. Be polite, respectful of the headliner (even if you don't love their music!), and chances are more shows will come your way. You may not be calling the shots, but you don't have to plan anything either—you just show up and play!

SETTING UP A GIG

So many crazy, spontaneous things happen at concerts that it's easy to overlook how much planning is involved. Before you commit to anything, make sure you have a solid plan in place.

RENTING A PA

Larger venues have their own PA, but you may need to rent one for unusual venues—like a record store or your backyard. If you're only expecting around twenty to fifty people, a simple PA will more than suffice (you don't want to blow their heads off!). You'll need:

· Two speakers, plus stands.

· Two to three monitors.

· Two to three microphones, plus stands.

· A four- to eight-channel mixing board.

OFF THE FLOOR

When a mixing board is small, your instruments will probably be "live off the floor." This means that any instrument with an amp won't have a microphone. Instead, all the mics will be used for vocals. Don't worry. If your amps are loud enough for your practice space, they should work here.

KEEP IT BALANCED

If you're going to put on a show that involves any renting—for the space or the PA—then you'll need a budget. This is a pretty simple equation. You just add up all of these things to get your costs. For example:

$100 for renting Louie's Café
+ $70 for the PA and mics
_____
= $170 cost!

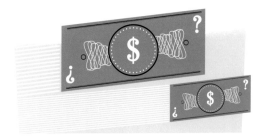

WHO'S PAYING FOR THIS?

While you and the bands should pay for everything, you can help cover your costs through your audience. After all, you are providing the entertainment!

KEEP IT COVERED

Welcome to the "cover charge." It gets its name because it's used to cover the costs of the show. Wanna know how much to charge? It's always a good idea not to be greedy. Divide your cost by the number of people you expect to come:

$170
÷ 40 people
_____
= $4.25 cover

This is the lowest cover you can charge without losing money.

GET SOME HELP

You'll be too busy performing to handle things like collecting cover charges. Ask a friend or family member to be the doorperson—they collect the money. Get a few people to share the responsibility so no one misses the whole show. You'll also need a soundperson to work the PA. Usually at small gigs, the musicians in the bands take turns doing sound for each other. But if you know someone who is eager to man the board for the show, then go for it. Chances are, that person is just as excited to experiment doing sound as you are to play!

OK, everything in place? Then let's have a great gig!

By the way, if you make more money than your costs, that's called profit. Don't keep it to yourself—spread it among the bands and staff. Well done!

CHECK 1 2 3!

The day of the show is here. Sweet. But before the audience can be let in, two things need to happen: *load-in,* where you bring your gear into the venue, and *soundcheck,* where you set up on stage and get proper volumes for the venue.

WHAT EXACTLY ARE WE CHECKING FOR?

Every venue sounds different from the last. Different room sizes, PA systems, microphones, even the building materials used to construct the room can change the way the band sounds. You need time to adjust everything before the crowd sees and hears you—this is what soundcheck is for. It's private time to get everything sounding perfect through the PA. If you just walked on stage and plugged in, it would sound *baaaaadddd.*

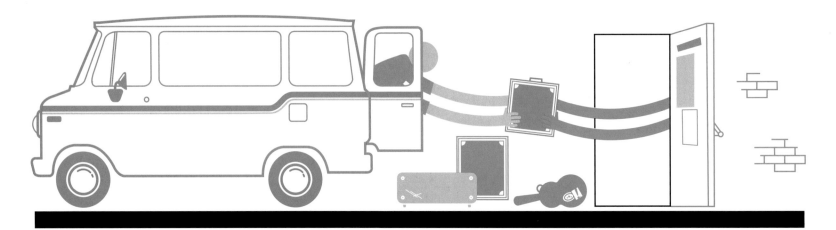

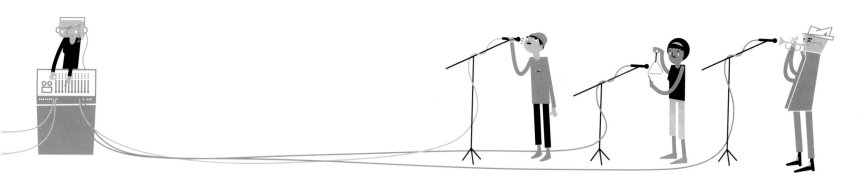

HONOR THY SOUNDPERSON

You always need to be kind to the soundperson—give this person a reason to dislike you, and your band's set will pay the price! Say hello, wait as things are set up, and do as you're told. He'll ask you to play one at a time, usually starting with the drummer. Just relax and be patient—the soundperson will make everything sound great!

TESTING...

Once the instruments are set up, it's time to play a test song. Choose one that everyone in the band feels comfy with. Listen for problems: can you hear all the instruments? Are any too loud? When the song is finished, ask the soundperson to make any necessary adjustments to monitors, whether it's a little more lead vocal or a little less guitar. Once everyone is happy with the sounds, you can relax and wait for showtime!

There's no time!

The first rule of any soundcheck is that the headliner gets the most time to work things out. If you're the opener—and especially if you are one of, say, five bands playing—you may not get a full soundcheck. Instead you'll get what's called a line check...in front of the crowd. Just before you start performing, the soundperson will ask each person to play his or her instrument for a few seconds. Then everyone starts playing the first song while the soundperson evens everything out. It's not ideal, but be understanding—the soundperson has a lot on the go, and if you complain, you'll likely have one rough-sounding show!

KEEPING YOUR COOL

Nerves are a big part of getting up on stage, and it's not just musicians who feel this way. Public speaking puts people's stomachs in knots, and even pro athletes feel edgy before the big game. So how do you keep the shakes and jitters from ruining your big moment?

MAKE A PRE-SHOW ROUTINE

Is it showtime yet? Yep, thought so. Must've been that twist in your stomach getting tighter! It's OK to be nervous—that just means you really care about how you sound. See, it's a good thing! Still, you don't want to be a wreck when you hit the stage. Sometimes, it helps to have a routine to relax you before you perform:

· Take a walk outside.

· Close your eyes, sit down, and meditate (just think relaxing thoughts).

· Stretch and jog on the spot (this will loosen you up!).

· Read a book or have a laugh with a friend.

IT'S ALL IN YOUR MIND

The best performances happen when you feel free of fear—and that's a tall order when you're in the midst of stage-fright panic! Once on stage, keep these nuggets of wisdom in your back pocket:

This is just one show—For the most part, one show won't make or break you, so stop putting so much importance on it!

That wasn't as bad as it seemed—Don't clench up if you make a mistake—chances are, you're the only person who noticed. Speaking of which...

Don't apologize!—When you say things from the stage like "Sorry we're playing so badly," it just confirms for everyone in the room that you are playing badly.

No one's recording this—Well, maybe someone is, but the great thing about live shows is that they can be forgotten—not like an album. So experiment and be free on stage.

And if things don't go the way you planned, there's always next time!

Remember what works for next time—The next day, talk with your band about the show. Did a particular song go really well? Did anything feel awkward? You can even ask a friend you trust about it. Whatever the case, use everyone's comments to make your next gig even better.

Do not open! Dark secret inside!

You think you can handle the truth? Seriously? Well, here it is. Somewhere along the way—could be your first gig, could be your one hundred and first—you will experience a show of such indescribable horror that you will want to crawl into a hole with a bag of licorice and never come out. Everything will go wrong. But it's not the end of the world. It happens to EVERYONE. Don't let it stop YOU from playing music again.

Slowly, Surely

Your first gig! Getting knots in your stomach just thinking about it? That's OK. Even big-name, show-stopping performers have felt like that too.

66 When Metric first started playing concerts I was very shy and nervous. It took a long time for me to gain confidence, but now performing is my favorite part of the musical process! Just remember that people love music, and they want to have a good time. Don't be afraid to be honest. 99

—*Emily Haines*
SINGER/KEYBOARDIST, METRIC

ALL SET?

Ever notice those pieces of paper on the stage? Those are setlists, the list of songs the band will play that night. A strong setlist helps the show run smoothly. It also helps the band control the audience's energy—pumping them up, then calming things down. Here are four tips for creating a great setlist:

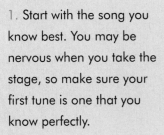

1. Start with the song you know best. You may be nervous when you take the stage, so make sure your first tune is one that you know perfectly.

2. Don't put too many slow songs in a row or your audience will lose interest. (Unless that's your band's sound. Then that's OK!)

3. Play your very best song last. End with a bang!

4. Keep it short. Your set should be about twenty-five to thirty minutes long. Better to leave your fans screaming for more than to watch them leave before you finish.

YOUR ABSOLUTE
LAST-MINUTE
PRE-GIG CHECKLIST!

- ☐ IS EVERYONE'S SETLIST WRITTEN AND ON STAGE?

- ☐ IS YOUR AMP/INSTRUMENT TURNED ON?

- ☐ ARE ALL YOUR VOLUME KNOBS AT THE PROPER SETTINGS?

- ☐ ARE THE MICROPHONE STANDS ADJUSTED TO THE RIGHT HEIGHT?

- ☐ DOES EVERYONE HAVE A BOTTLE OF WATER? (IT GETS HOT UP THERE!)

- ☐ DO THE GUITARISTS HAVE EXTRA PICKS?

- ☐ DOES THE DRUMMER HAVE EXTRA DRUMSTICKS?

- ☐ ARE ALL OF THE INSTRUMENTS TUNED?

PLAYLIST
It's A-Live!

A frontperson with a lot of charisma can really make a great show even better. Hunt down the live performances of these tunes and compare them to their studio versions to hear how the performance really comes alive!

THE FLAMING LIPS » "RACE FOR THE PRIZE" AT COACHELLA 2004 (VIDEO)

Lead singer Wayne Coyne starts things off by getting inside a giant clear ball and rolling himself out over the crowd like a hamster!

QUEEN » "WE ARE THE CHAMPIONS" AT LIVE AID 1985 (VIDEO)

Already a stunning song, but watch this to see one hundred thousand people eating out of the late Freddie Mercury's hand. Truly royal.

SAM COOKE » LIVE AT THE HARLEM SQUARE CLUB, 1963

Mr. Cooke spent his youth singing gospel shows, and you can feel it in the devotion he gives to this performance.

THE STAGE *is* SET

Playing live is all about being viewed and heard by an audience. That's where the stage and the sound equipment come in. The stage's job is to display the band for everyone to see. There are all sorts of stages out there—from those massive amphitheaters to tiny raised platforms found in the corner of a club. Big or small, most of them follow the same basic layout.

1 STAGE

The stage itself is a platform, usually made of wood or metal. It's sometimes covered with a thin carpet or other non-slip covering.

2 MICROPHONES

Mics are placed as close as possible to amps and instruments so they can capture the sound. The mics, amps, and monitors together form the PA system.

3 DIRECT BOX

Some instruments, such as keyboards, sound great through a little device called a direct box (DI). The DI is used instead of a mic, and connects right into the instrument.

4 MAINS

These large speakers allow the audience to hear the band playing.

5 MONITORS

These speakers are placed on stage to let the musicians hear the rest of the band clearly. Vocals are always put through the monitors, as are acoustic instruments, because they don't use any amplification. Monitors are often called wedges, because the speakers are, well, wedge-shaped!

6 SOUNDBOARD

The mics and DIs are all connected to a mixing board that is manned by the soundperson. The soundperson controls how all of the instruments on stage sound through the mains.

7 LIGHTS

Nothing lets you know it's showtime like a half-dozen giant lights in your face. (Those lights are hot, so get ready to sweat!)

My Life on the Road

While it's nothing that anyone should rush into—it's expensive and requires a lot of planning—touring is super fun.

Why did I like touring so much? Because I got to meet new people all the time and visit parts of the world I'd never seen before, and the band picked up new fans wherever we went. The times that stand out the most for me are these three "pinch me I must be dreaming" moments. Drumroll, please…

Top 3 Favorite Tour Moments

#3 The band traveled forty-eight hours (including two long bus rides and four plane trips) to get to and from Japan to play the Fuji Rock Festival. We arrived in the middle of the night and woke up early the next morning to do interviews. Then we were playing an afternoon show in front of about ten thousand people. Right after, it was back on the bus to the Tokyo airport, where another plane would take us to L.A.! Thousands of miles from home, no real sleep, all to take the stage for only forty-five minutes—but it was so worthwhile. The crowd went completely nuts—clapping, cheering, screaming, and singing from the moment we hit the stage. Afterward, we were mobbed like pop stars. Crazy!

#2 We were the second-last band on the final night of the Lollapalooza Festival in Grant Park on Chicago's waterfront.

Before us was Queens of the Stone Age (a personal fave!), after us was Red Hot Chili Peppers (whose early records I grew up learning how to play drums to!). The schedule was very tight—we had only about forty-five minutes to play. But our show was so well received that after we finished, the crowd simply would not stop cheering for an encore. Chants from the crowd went from "ONE MORE SONG!" to "WE'RE NOT LEAVING!" Even though we didn't get an encore in the end, the five minutes of deafening cheering and chanting for us— all while one of the biggest bands in the world was waiting to take the stage—is something I'll never forget. Awesome!

#1 (Caution: this one's a little mushy!) OK, so we're playing in Indio, California—a lush, green oasis in the middle of the barren, dusty desert—at a world-famous rock festival. This was pretty much the biggest show I'd played yet. I'd just

had my thirtieth birthday two days before, and my girlfriend had flown in to help me celebrate. From the first chord, the entire band was sweating buckets, but for me, it was about more than the 110-degree sun. I was more nervous than I could ever remember. That's because just before the last song, I walked up to mic and, in front of about ten thousand people, asked my girlfriend to marry me! (OK, I'll wait for you to stop barfing...All done?) The best part about it was how I was able to turn a moment that was all about me and my band into a chance to celebrate someone who is really special to me.

CHAPTER 5

Keep a Record

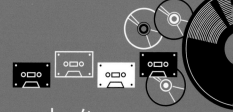

"Do I really sound like that?" Well, maybe you do, maybe you don't. But that's not the point. Recording is about making things sound the way you want them to, not the way they do.

There's a reason why The Beatles quit playing live concerts in 1966, at the height of their popularity. It was so they could concentrate on recording. A recording studio is pretty much a playground for curious musicians. In a studio, musicians can explore new sounds and experiment with their songs in exciting ways.

Of course, professional studios can be VERY expensive places. A single day can cost hundreds, even thousands of dollars! From Fleetwood Mac all the way up to the last Guns N' Roses album, music history is full of tales of bands spending millions of dollars and years in the studio trying to perfect their albums. Yikes! Who can afford that? Oh yeah, rock stars.

Fortunately, that's not something you need to worry about. Recording has come a long way. Today's computers are a few small adjustments away from being your own personal studio—some are practically ready to go out of the box. You may not quite get the sounds you hear on your favourite albums at home, but you'll be amazed at just how much you *can* do. It's all about experimenting and taking chances. It doesn't even have to be a song. If you have an idea—any idea—then you should try it out!

What Is Recording, Really?

Recording is the act of capturing sounds and storing them so you can listen to them later. But hey, you knew that, since things get recorded all the time, like messages from your friends on a cell phone. You don't care how that message sounds—as long as you know that your friend is coming at 4:30, you're cool. But music is different. It needs to sound good.

TOGETHER AND ALONE

What makes recording music so difficult is that every instrument has its own personality. Some are loud and deep, others are quiet and thin. If you put a full band in a room and try to record it with one mic, it'll sound like a room full of people all shouting at once. But if you record each musician separately, you can pay attention to each instrument's own personality and adjust the sound until it's great, both on its own and with the rest of the band.

Quick guide to home recording

Here it is, a very simple intro to how music recording works. There's so much more to learn, but everything you need to start is right here!

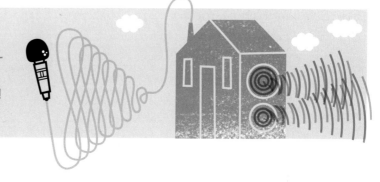

LAYER BY LAYER

When making an album, each instrument is recorded to its own channel, called a track. Each track needs its own microphone. When the band plays together in a room, unwanted sounds from other instruments are picked up by the mics. This is called bleed. To record the entire band without lots of bleed, each member plays one at a time.

Put your favorite song on right now. Can you identify the instruments? Imagine each one as a different colored blanket. The art of recording is taking all of those blankets and laying them perfectly on top of each other. Sounds simple...

1. Usually, the first person recorded is the drummer—it's the drummer's beat that keeps time for the song.

2. Then the bass player records over the beat...

3. Next, the guitarist...

4. And finally, the lead singer!

INSIDE *the* PROFESSIONAL STUDIO

Even if it's years before you get to use one, there's no harm in seeing how a professional studio is put together. There's a reason why people still pay big bucks to use them. They're perfectly designed to capture excellent sounds of all sorts of instruments quickly. Many also have an arsenal of instruments and amps to give your song that little something extra.

1 The music is captured by microphones as it's played.

2 Microphones placed near the instrument are called close mics.

3 Room mics capture sound from farther away.

4 The music travels from the mics into the control room through long wires called cables.

5 The control room is the cockpit of a studio. All the important recording devices are in here.

6 This wall of gadgets is full of preamps. A preamp is used to adjust and improve an instrument's sound as it's recorded.

7 The live room is where the bands play as they're recorded, especially on instruments like drums.

8 Isolation booths are soundproof rooms that allow players to perform together but record all their instruments separately.

9 Everyone hears each other's instruments through headphones.

10 Studio walls are thick. They often have an open space in the middle that blocks even more sound from other rooms.

11 An amp box is like an isolation booth, except it's just big enough to hold an amp.

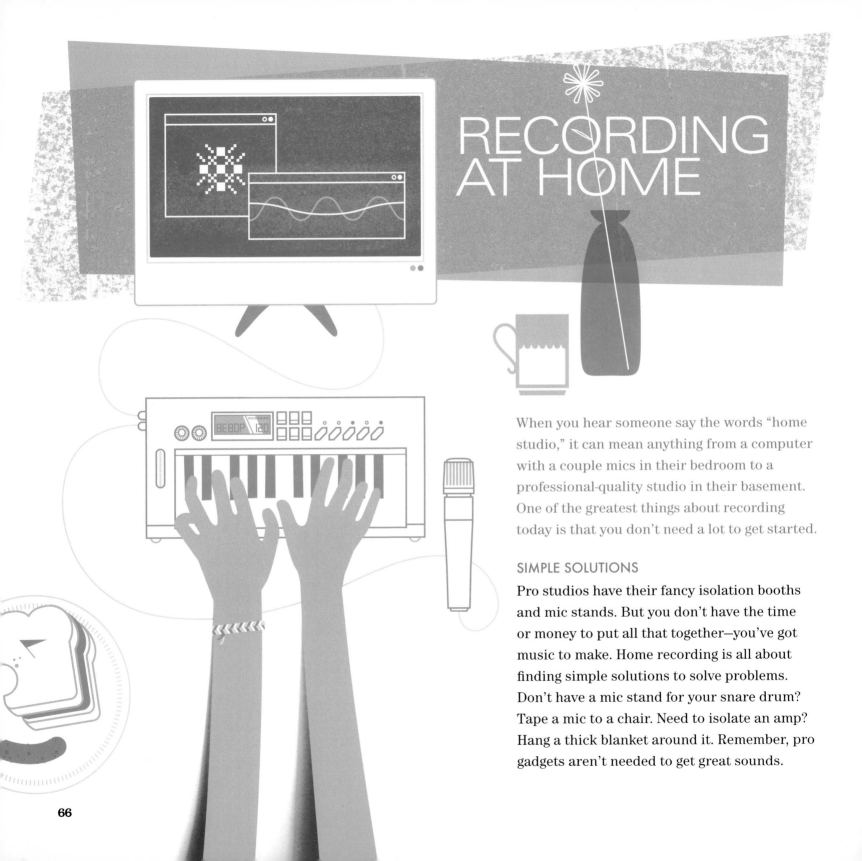

RECORDING AT HOME

When you hear someone say the words "home studio," it can mean anything from a computer with a couple mics in their bedroom to a professional-quality studio in their basement. One of the greatest things about recording today is that you don't need a lot to get started.

SIMPLE SOLUTIONS

Pro studios have their fancy isolation booths and mic stands. But you don't have the time or money to put all that together—you've got music to make. Home recording is all about finding simple solutions to solve problems. Don't have a mic stand for your snare drum? Tape a mic to a chair. Need to isolate an amp? Hang a thick blanket around it. Remember, pro gadgets aren't needed to get great sounds.

THE FRUGAL FOUR

These four items are the cheapest and best way to make your own super-cool home studio:

1 Recording software—There are lots of types out there, and more being developed all the time.

2 A Shure SM-57 or -58 dynamic microphone—For about a hundred dollars, you can get the same mics used in studios. They capture sound from close up and are great for vocals, guitar amps, and snare drums.

3 Interface—This device lets you connect your mics to your computer.

4 PZM or boundary microphone —These small mics are placed on the floor or hung on a wall, where they can take in sound from big instruments like drums and pianos. If money is tight, this mic is the least important.

Electric company

People have been making music on computers for a pretty long time. Today's recording programs owe a lot to electronic pioneers like Kraftwerk or Raymond Scott, who wanted to see what would happen if a computer was programmed to make sounds instead of solving giant math equations. The guiding force behind electronic music is the loop. The loop is a repeating phrase over which other sounds are placed—think of it as the computer's drumbeat or rhythm guitar.

News Flash!

Getting your start in recording doesn't have to involve music—there are all kinds of skits and bits you can lay down to experiment with capturing sounds.

66 When I was twelve or so, I started making pretend radio shows with my friends and cousins. We'd pick music and do the news and weather, and record it all on a crappy tape recorder. 99

—*Buck 65*

Tricks

OF THE

Trade

If recording really turns your crank, it won't take long for you to want to try something more than just sticking a microphone in front of an instrument and pressing Record. Well, OK then, let's see what we can do about that.

COOL SOUNDS

Capturing sounds is about messing around until you find what you're looking for. Recording engineers have tried everything from sticking a mic in a clothes dryer and using it as a drum to recording vocals while sitting in a giant satellite dish!

THE PERFECT PLACE

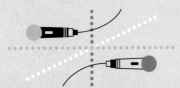

A mic captures sound differently depending on where it is. Try recording an instrument with a mic a few steps away, then try it on the other side of the room. The farther away your mic is, the more distant and echo-ey your instrument sounds.

HEARING DOUBLE

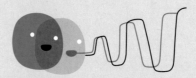

To get a more powerful sound from vocals or guitars, try doubling. Record the vocal or instrument on one track, and then record the exact same thing on another track. Make the performances as identical as possible for the best effect.

DIFFERENT ROOMS, DIFFERENT SOUNDS

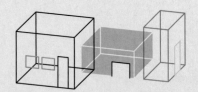

Try recording in different rooms. Room shapes and surfaces all change sound. Absorbent surfaces, like carpet and blankets, trap sound to give you a pure tone. Reflective surfaces, like tiles or windows, bounce sound around.

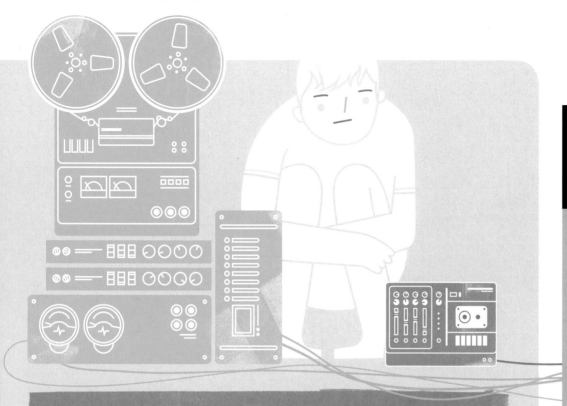

HI-FI VERSUS LO-FI

You might have heard of the term "hi-fi." It stands for "high fidelity," which means something that sounds as good as possible. For most people, this is the goal of recording. But in the late 1980s and 1990s, many musicians didn't have the money for expensive studios. Instead they used four-track cassette recorders to make albums at home. The result was dirty and noisy, but suited the songs. These home-recorded albums were called lo-fi. Today, lo-fi sounds are used not just because it's cheap, but because it's sometimes the best sound for the song.

PLAYLIST
Sounds Good

Sound quality can have a great impact on how your song is heard, but "best quality" isn't always the best way to go. Some musicians even mix both hi- and lo-fi sounds together.

GUIDED BY VOICES » "SMOTHERED IN HUGS"

There's nothing hi-fi about this tune. Its dirtiness makes the song's great melody sound sloppy and sticky, like maple syrup!

COLDPLAY » "VIVA LA VIDA"

It doesn't get any clearer and crisper than Coldplay. They use the latest technology to make sure every last harmony and bell of this hopeful tune ring true.

M.I.A. » "PAPER PLANES"

The first time you hear this track's trashy samples, you'll see they completely stand out from the punchy basslines and beats. The combo is dramatic and hooks you instantly.

CHAPTER 6

Spread the Word

Did you put up the posters? Ah, man! What about the website—are the new dates posted yet? Did you remember to pick up the T-shirts? What do you mean the design isn't finalized? I was supposed to do that?

Bands can put so much pressure on themselves to promote their music that it's easy to forget that making things like posters, T-shirts, and album covers is also a lot of fun. All of this stuff is art, and just like music itself, it feels great to create. Seeing someone walking down the street in your band's T-shirt? Well, that feels pretty cool too!

The bottom line is that you can do anything to promote your band—the more original, the better. Musicians make everything from videos and websites to handbags and underwear to get their name out there. A Welsh band named Super Furry Animals even bought a tank, painted it blue, and drove it around to English music festivals with music blaring out of it! That's crazy, right!? So you see, there's no such thing as a bad idea.

Maybe you can't afford to buy a tank, but with a little creativity and some help from your friends, you can really get the word out. So are you feeling game? Then let's get people talking!

MAXIMUM COVERAGE

Art is used everywhere in music—it's a big part of a band's image. Whether your music is wild and silly or dark and deep, that image says a lot about about how your fans will relate to you.

YOU KNOW MY NAME...

Nothing says a band's image like a logo (the way their band name is written). Punk, metal, and hip hop bands are really well known for having easily recognizable logos. More than anything, the logo should reinforce your sound, whether playful or serious.

DOES A COVER MATTER?

Just because lots of people buy their music digitally, it doesn't mean that an album's cover isn't important. A killer cover completes the experience of listening to an album. When figuring out your cover, try to think about what your music "looks" like. Is it blue? Green? Is it an animal or a large building? It might seem a little weird, but thinking like this can really help you come up with an image that suits your songs.

GETTING INSPIRED

If you need a little help coming up with ideas for a cover, take a look at some others that you really like, and not just album covers either—magazines, cereal boxes, anything can work. Look carefully at how the images and text are placed. Many albums use artwork that is meant to look like a small book. They'll do things like list the band's name like an author's, or list songs like a table of contents. It's just a way of saying, "These aren't just songs, they're little stories, too."

POSTER
PERFECT

Rock 'n' roll is the perfect world for posters—in fact, many artists have made their name designing them for concerts. Here are two ways to make great posters:

Put the names of the bands playing a show really big, like this:

Be creative and make something curious that causes people to look closer.

FRIDAY, OCTOBER 1

RUNNING DUCK
THE FOREST
AT NIGHT
JASON
EVANS

FIVE DOLLARS

the
SNOOZE
BUTTONS

These posters are tough to pull off, but they're the kind that fans want to put on their bedroom walls after the show!

One Great Cover

Every cover starts with a great image, even if that "image" is little more than a lot of really large words. But where does the idea for that image come from?

"Every musician and band is different, and every album is different, so there's no real formula for making a great cover. You just have to find a concept that works with the music and be consistent. Ask a lot of questions."

—Louise Upperton
ALBUM COVER DESIGNER

IT LOOKS *good* ON YOU

If we have to wear clothes—and thankfully, yes we do—then most of us would rather those clothes say something about us. That's what makes the band shirt perfect for spreading the word. But heck, you already know this—chances are, you're wearing a shirt with a fave cartoon/actor/athlete/rockstar on it right now! With a few blank shirts and some supplies, you can create a T-shirt with your band logo on it too!

You'll need:
· Plain T-shirts in any color
· Pieces of cardboard
· Paper
· T-shirt paint in desired colors
· Pen or pencil
· Scissors or utility knife

The Stencil Shirt

Most indie bands get a professional to make their T-shirts using a process called silk-screening. While it is possible to do silk-screening at home, it can be a little complex and requires specific chemicals. A great way around this problem is to use T-shirt paint and homemade stencils! The paint is cheap and the stencils are easy to make.

Step 1

Sketch some designs on a piece of paper. When you have something that you like, move on. Make sure your design isn't too complex.

Step 2

Draw your finished design on a piece of cardboard and cut it out. This is your T-shirt stencil.

Step 3

Place a T-shirt on a table and tape down the corners so it doesn't move. Lay the stencil on the shirt where you want the design to go.

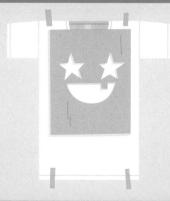

Step 4

Paint inside the stencil on the fabric. Be sure to paint right to the edges so that you fill in the stencil completely.

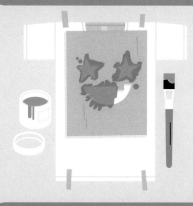

Step 5

Remove the stencil. Be careful not to smudge the paint. Lay the T-shirt flat so it can dry.

Step 6

For a really cool trick, repeat steps 3 to 5 with another stencil and another color on your dried T-shirt. This will make a layered design.

Step 7

Repeat with as many shirts as you like!

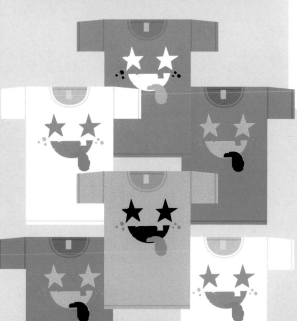

Quick tip: The order in which you paint each stencil is important! Whatever color needs to go on the bottom must be painted first. For more complex designs, test your stencils on a blank sheet of paper first. Once you paint on a shirt, it's there forever.

Network It, Baby!

Promotion used to be all about getting major labels to spend thousands of dollars on ads—which the band would later have to pay back with money they made off album sales. Yuck! Thankfully, today you can do so much for free. No promotional tool is easier to use and can reach as many people as a website. From the world's biggest bands to ones just starting out, everyone uses them.

IT'S GOT EVERYTHING

You probably don't need me to tell you why a website is great, but in short, it's got everything. Your website can include photos, gig dates, news, blogs, and of course, music. More than that, people *expect* that you'll have a website for your band—it's just as important as your first show. Lots of bands have their own web addresses, or domains, but setting one up costs money. Why bother with that when the most effective music websites today are free?

FREE FOR YOU AND ME

The Internet moves pretty fast—what's hot one week can be stone cold the next. Whatever the hot free web-network is, it will help you get the word out. So make sure you keep up!

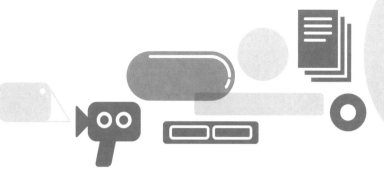

WHAT SHOULD I POST?

What makes a free site great is that it lets people hear your music right away. So when starting your own page, it's probably a good idea to get a little something recorded first. Think about it this way: What's easier to understand—reading about music or listening to it? Exactly!

POST OFTEN

It's a good thing that web pages are so easy to use because you need to post stuff A LOT. Try posting something about your group at least once a week—a new photo, a short video of you practicing, info about a song in progress, stuff like that. Fans will come back often so they don't miss anything. And if you're the outspoken type, you might even want to start your own blog.

Keep it safe

The web is an awesome tool, but it's also filled with a few dangers, even for adults. No matter what your music sounds like, chances are someone will eventually send you a message offering to help promote your music or put on a show. Never agree to meet someone you were introduced to through a website or give out any of your personal information.

Beautiful
COMMERCIALS

Music videos can be very expensive—it's pretty common for a band to spend three times what they did on their entire album to make one little video! Not only that, their song will often have to be edited—or made shorter—to get more airplay on TV. And today, even music channels are playing fewer videos every year. So why would anyone make a video at all?

AS YOU LIKE IT

Well, for starters, a video is a kind of commercial for your band, and it can help you reach new fans. Videos may be off TV, but they're all over the Internet and on DVDs, which means people can watch their favorite bands whenever they like. And let's not forget that many musicians consider videos as much a piece of art as their music. Since bands no longer have to worry about what TV stations will air, they can make exactly the video they want to make!

TREAT YOU RIGHT

All pro videos begin with a written proposal called a treatment. The director listens to the song and writes a detailed plan for a video. If the band—and record company—likes what it reads, then it's time to get started! Many videos are mostly performance footage, of the band either on stage or in some location like a warehouse, beach, street corner, or forest. That's OK, but the most interesting videos are the ones that find a way to blend a unique story into the band's song.

NOT ALWAYS LITERAL

Part of the reason some directors are so successful is that they are not literal in how they interpret a song.

A literal interpretation means images that say exactly what the lyrics do. If the song says, "Susie got up and made some tea/checked the papers, called her family," then you would get an actress to be Susie and show her making tea, reading the newspaper, and calling her parents.

But an imaginative director can come up with a story based on how the music sounds, not what the lyrics say. For example, maybe this song is a really energetic track—so Susie is drinking tea while flying in a speeding spaceship. Now that's fun to watch!

ACTION!

The director films many short segments called shots. Each shot may be just seconds long, but the director often requests numerous attempts, or takes, to get the best performance. Once the filming is complete, the director views all of the takes and picks the best ones to create a full video.

CUTS

Music videos are known for having lots of cuts. A cut is the point where a video moves from one shot to another. One second you're watching the drummer, and the next, an eagle swooping down. Having lots of cuts lets the director move from one band member to the next—or back and forth between storylines—quickly. Each cut usually happens in time to a part of the music, such as when a drum is hit.

No Experience Necessary

It isn't just big-time directors who make great music videos. Lots of other people have too. Here's an example of a self-taught musician turned director who watched and learned.

66 With digital cameras you don't need a big budget—all you need is a great idea, a bunch of friends, and some lights. Filmmakers like Spike Jonze set a very easy but creative standard with videos like 'Praise You' by Fatboy Slim. 99

—*Kevin Drew*
SINGER/GUITARIST, BROKEN SOCIAL SCENE

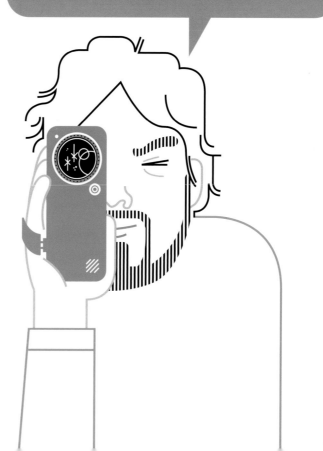

Christopher Mills's Guide to
MAKING A VIDEO

Our expert video director Christopher Mills, who was nominated for an MTV award for his clip for Modest Mouse's "Float On," is here to show you how to bring your ideas to the screen using a regular digital video camera. You don't need a lot of money, just some friends to help out.

LEARN HOW TO FILM THINGS INTERESTINGLY

Take pictures of EVERYTHING! Spend some time with a still camera, a video camera, your sketchbook, or even just your imagination, and find ways to make everything you see look interesting.

COMBINE VISUAL IDEAS

Decide what looks good when you film it. You know that it looks really great when someone does a windmill guitar move. Now play with the camera and figure out how to translate that to a lens. For example, "It looks really cool when I put my camera down low and see my friend up against the sky with clouds behind him and a storm's brewing and he does a windmill guitar move!"

IMAGINE IMAGES THAT MATCH THE SONG

If you hear a loud drumbeat, it might make you think about an elephant walking down the street. Try to figure out how to translate that idea into something you can do with your friends—like putting them in elephant costumes.

Stay in sync

One way that directors get the music you hear in the video to match what the musicians are playing is to have them play the song on set while filming. Then, when the director gets back to the studio, they match the video to a high-quality audio of the song. After everything is matched, the sound from the filming is turned off and—*voila*—the song and film are perfectly combined.

TAKE YOUR IMAGES AND LAY OUT A SCRIPT

Take the song's lyrics, put them on one side of the page, and write or draw what happens for each of those parts in the song on the other side of the page. Then once you have what happens laid out in the script, you can figure out, "OK, I need an elephant for this thing!"

PLAYLIST
Stay Curious

The list could go on forever, but these videos really stand out as great examples of what you can do with a camera, a great song, and an open mind.

BJÖRK » "HUMAN BEHAVIOUR"

Director Michel Gondry is a wacky video genius, and Björk has inspired him to do some of his best work. This fantastic journey of Björk and a teddy bear in the woods remains the best of the bunch.

SINEAD O'CONNOR » "NOTHING COMPARES TO YOU"

OK, this is a bit of a video oldie, but it shows that a really good performance—and a well-timed tear—can be just as good as a whole pile of crazy effects.

OK GO » "HERE IT GOES AGAIN"

This odd little video is a great example of how fast a video can make a band well known. It features the band members on treadmills!

BLUR » "COFFEE & TV"

The story in this video doesn't really have much to do with the song, but that poor lost milk carton is so adorable. Don't you just love him?

Mixing BUSINESS with PLEASURE

"I love music, but I don't enjoy being on stage."

Sound familiar? If you're music-obsessed there are many ways to be involved without actually being a musician. Lots of people work as managers, club owners, and label reps. The fact is, these people are really important for getting great music heard by the public. Here are the main players in the biz:

Booking agents—They put together tours for musicians. They work with local promoters who help bring bands to their town.

Managers—They help bands organize all the little day-to-day details, from tour schedules to promotion to paperwork.

Producers—They work with musicians during recording sessions to make the best-sounding album possible.

Record label owners—Help musicians create, release, and promote music.

IF YOU BUILD IT, THEY WILL COME

You've all heard or seen people who make it big by going on TV or being "discovered," but there's more than one way to make it in the music business. There are lots of little music communities out there, and you can build your own. Lots of people call this being indie—short for "independent." It's not just musicians who are indie. Some record stores, instrument shops, and record labels are too. They all build and belong to a music community. In short, being indie means that if you're friendly and helpful to musicians, clubs, labels, and stores, these people will help you out, too. And when you're trying to find your way as a musician, the help of a strong community goes a long way.

It's My Job!

The joy of being in the music biz is that even though you may not get the same props as the performers, deep down good musicians know they need you more than you need them!

> **"** I used to be the guy in the hall at school turning his friends on to new bands by handing out mix tapes and CDs. Today, I basically do the same thing, except the bands are on my own label and I get paid to spread the word. **"**
>
> —*Joel Carriere*
> **BAND MANAGER/RECORD-LABEL OWNER**

Hey Music, Wait Up!

So that's it—the basics of what I've learned so far as a musician. Or, well, most of it. I'm still learning. Back at school, I was known as a bit of a music expert, and I bought right into that role. I knew my stuff, and after just one listen, I could easily separate the good bands from the bad. Or so I thought. But then, a couple of years later, I'd hear the same "bad" groups again and wonder why I didn't like them in the first place. After that happened a few times, I started to realize that music was just waiting for *me* to catch up to *it*. It still is today, even when I'm a little slow to figure out what it's trying to tell me. That's why I still look forward to discovering new tunes. And why it's always a surprise to hear what others have to say through music. Who knows, maybe the next great song I hear will be yours!

BAND NOTES
YOUR SECRET STYLE FILES

From drums to pianos, trumpets to your own voice, every instrument has something unique to offer a musician. But the real trick is finding that bit of yourself in the instrument you play.

Within each instrument are tons of secret styles of playing—maybe even some not yet discovered—that allow you to become more than just another musician. They let you say what's most important to you with music. And nothing you can do with an instrument is more fun or meaningful than that!

So let's break it down…

· Amps
· Bass
· Drums
· Electronics
· Guitar

· Horns
· Keyboards
· Strings
· Vocals

AMPS & EFFECTS
If it's not broke, you can break it!

There are two main types of instruments out there. Acoustic instruments, like horns, strings, drums, and pianos, can be heard on their own. But electric instruments, like electric guitars, bass, and keyboards, need an amp to be heard. Amp stands for amplifier, and it's as big a part of your sound as the instrument itself. But what would you say if I told you that the best way to use your amp…is to break it?

Break it in!

Nearly all amps come with two volume knobs—the gain and the master. The gain is how much sound is coming out of your instrument and into the amp. The master is the sound level of the amp itself.

So how does this "break" your amp? Breaking just refers to the way that the sound gets all crunchy as the amp is turned up. Technically, this distortion is the sound of the volume being too loud for the amp's circuits to provide a pure, clear tone. Guitarists in particular love this tone, or sound.

Try this: With your gain low, you can turn the master up really high and still get a clean tone. Now crank up your gain and listen as the sound begins to break! Play with these knobs to discover all the sounds you can get.

Positive feedback

Feedback is the crazy wail that comes from an amp when it's cranked up really loud. On a vocal mic, the sound is shrill and annoying—you might know it best as the "WOOO" sound that accompanies your principal's speeches at assemblies. But on a guitar, it's wild, loud, and totally rules.

Try this: Turn your amp up to about 7 and stand a few feet away, facing it. A low howl should start to build and gain in volume. If it's happening too quickly or too slowly, adjust either your distance from the amp or the volume. When you get some feedback going, move, twist, and shake your guitar and listen to how the sound changes!

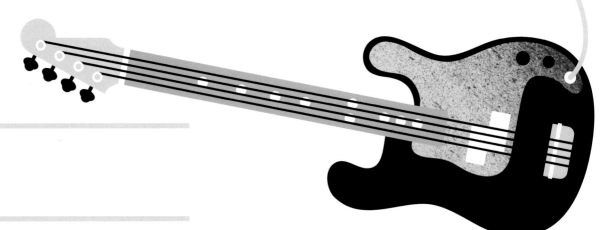

BASS
The unsung hero

One of the biggest lies you'll ever hear about the bass guitar is that it's easy. With only four strings and no real chords, understanding how to play bass is pretty basic, but knowing how it fits into a band is totally different. In many ways, this is the instrument that controls the song.

Expert tip #1: As bass player, your job is to leave enough space for the other instruments to breathe. Try not to be the loudest instrument, unless you're in a reggae band—at that point, be loud and proud.

Expert tip #2: Don't wear your bass strap too low or you'll end up hurting yourself. You can't play as well when you can't reach the strings...unless you're Dee Dee Ramone!

—*Brendan Canning,* BROKEN SOCIAL SCENE

Can you feel it?

Imagine it this way. High notes—like the ones that usually come from guitars, horns, or vocals—hit your ears directly. But low notes from a bass guitar are more "felt" than heard. The bass has a direct line to the feet and guts. Without thinking about it, you will move to the bass in a song. Just as a cobra dances with a snake charmer—only without the nasty fangs.

Expert tip: Use baby powder to slide up and down the neck. I love to use the low E string when I play, and when you're on a hot stage, this is the only way!

—*Melissa Auf der Maur,* BASSIST/SINGER, AUF DER MAUR, (FORMERLY OF SMASHING PUMPKINS AND HOLE)

DRUMS
The paranormal paradiddle

Paradiddles teach drummers coordination and balance. They're simply the patterns that most drum students learn first. There are dozens of different ones, but most are played using a single drum. As boring as these little exercises may be, practicing them can really pay off.

> **Try this:** A really basic paradiddle looks like this: LRLRLLRLRLRR. The "L" means you hit with your left hand and the "R" means your right—go on, try it out.

Think differently

Every instrument has some version of the paradiddle—on most instruments, it's scales. Yes, they're repetitive and boring, but they teach our hands, feet, and voices to do greater things later on. Remember, just because you do an exercise one way in practice, doesn't mean you can't experiment with that technique anyway you like on your own time!

> **Expert tip #1:** You can use duct tape on the head and bottom of your drums to eliminate ugly ringing tones.
>
> **Expert tip #2:** Adjust your snare and stool so that when you come down on your snare, your hand doesn't touch your leg. This can cause discomfort in the future, when playing harder and faster songs.
>
> —*Justin Peroff*, BROKEN SOCIAL SCENE

> **Try this:** Instead of playing a paradiddle on just one drum, play the pattern moving around the hi-hats, snare, and toms. This style lets you explore beats with a far different flavor than found on your standard rock or waltz beat.

ELECTRONICS
Loop-da-loop!

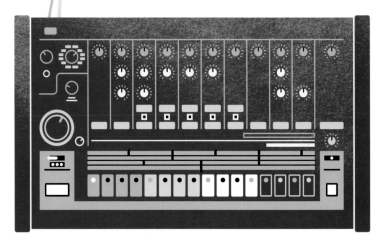

Computers are like any instrument—they still need a person to come up with the ideas and turn them into a song. But computers let us do things that are impossible on other instruments. Maybe one of the simplest and most beautiful things they can do is the loop—a series of sounds that repeats over and over again.

Around and around again

Loops are found everywhere today—in hip hop, dance music, pop songs, or experimental music. You can use a loop to keep a beat or to add an interesting background texture to a song (called ambience). That's just a fancy way of saying that the loop sits "behind" the song, like the background on a painting.

Try this: Use a loop made up of hundreds of singing voices or gently plucking violins to add atmosphere to your song.

You're loopy!

Loops are all about experimenting and having fun. To make a loop, start by recording some sounds—like birds chirping or someone talking. Then you can record more layers on top of it to create a unique series of noises! As these layers come together, even unmusical things start to sound musical!

Expert tip: Look at everything that exists as a musical instrument. I've used toy instruments and cardboard boxes in songs. I've even used the sound of a basketball bouncing on the floor for a bass drum.

—Buck 65

GUITAR
Name that tuning

In a lot of ways the guitar is the most overused, boring instrument out there—it's everywhere! Why so popular? It is easy to learn, thanks to the frets that show you where your fingers go. But let's face it, people love the guitar because it can do anything. No other instrument can be so light and fragile one moment and so ferocious and heavy the next. There are lots of ways to change your sound using different amps or guitar pedals, but one of the most underused ways is through alternate tunings.

A different tune
Most guitars are tuned to what is called standard tuning, or (from low string to high) E A D G B E. But there are dozens of guitar tunings out there. Why? Because a different tuning lets you get new voicing, or ways of "saying" a chord. Imagine voicing as someone's accent when they speak. Change the voicing on your guitar and suddenly it sounds Australian! Not really, but you get the idea. Remember, if it sounds right to you, that's all that matters.

Try this: Half step down—E♭, A♭, D♭, G♭, B♭, E♭

Tune the E-string down to E♭ and so on. This'll give you a heavier sound.

Try this: Drop D—D A D G B E

By just dropping the E-string down to a D, you can play super power chords by pressing the bottom three strings with one finger. Heavy!

Try this: Open G—D G D G B D

This is just one example of an open tuning. You can play a full chord without holding down any strings! While you strum the open chord, pick a random string and play notes up and down the neck. What do you find?

Expert tip: The best thing you could possibly do is learn to play every single melody you hear. Watch TV with your guitar, learn all the commercial jingles and all the theme songs. You are training your ear.

—Andrew Whiteman, BROKEN SOCIAL SCENE

HORNS
More than just hot air

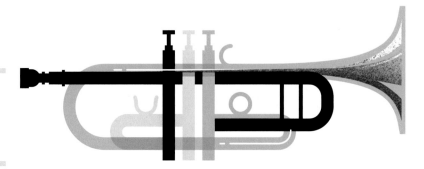

Horns are the pickles and onions to rock 'n' roll's burger. Add them to a song and a tasty thing gets a whole lot tastier. Horns are also called brass, and the most common ones you'll hear in a rock band are trumpets and saxophones. Brass work best when responding to the needs of a song. In other words, instead of writing a song on the horn, use one to make a pretty good song really great.

Trumpet—hear ye, hear ye!

Kings, queens, and armies all used trumpets to make big announcements—that's because these horns have a very high range and they can get really loud. It's the ideal instrument to really kick a song up a notch. Trumpet lines often happen in choruses or at the start or end of a song. You'll be amazed at how much more exciting a song's climax can sound when trumpets are added.

Try this: A trumpet can also be tender and mellow. To make your trumpet sound sad, cup your hand over the bell of the horn and pull it on and off as you play.

Saxophone—the wild one

Technically the saxophone is in the woodwind category because it requires a reed to play it. But in a lot of rock 'n' roll oufits they fall in with the brass. When most people are learning to play sax, they get frustrated by all the nasty squeals and squawks they get. But those crazy sounds come in handy when putting together a truly killer sax solo—some players call this sound skronk. It's kind of a made-up word, but what it's trying to say is that sometimes, the wrong sound is the right one.

Try this: Match a saxophone with a bassline or a guitar riff—everything sounds thicker and stronger.

Expert tip: Whatever town I'm stopped in, I find extra horn players to play with. With a horn section, the more the merrier!

—*Charles Spearin,* BROKEN SOCIAL SCENE

KEYBOARDS
The chameleon

The term "keyboard" means pretty much any instrument that is played by pressing those black and white keys you see on a piano. Organs, electric pianos, synthesizers—these are all keyboards. They come in all sizes and styles, but two things most have in common are range and change. The range refers to the number of notes they can play, from very high to very low. But what makes them really special is their ability to change their sound at the push of a button.

I hear VOICES!

Organs and electric pianos usually have only a few "voices," or different types of sounds they can make. But a synthesizer can have hundreds! Synthesizer loosely means "to copy," and that's what synths do—they copy sounds. Synths come with a bunch of built-in sounds called presets. Each preset is designed to imitate some sound, whether it's a real instrument or something imaginary—like an alien spaceship!

Highs and lows

Synths have so many sounds at their disposal that it's easy to get distracted making the craziest noises possible. It's helpful to remember that most keyboard parts still need some kind of melody to work. Keyboards are super versatile—you can play chords like a rhythm guitarist would, pump out a ridiculously low, feel-it-in-your-gut bassline, and then play a great little melody like a trumpet. All in the same song!

Try this: Don't get trapped into doing the same things in every song. You play an amazing instrument. Show everyone what it can do!

Expert tip: Be prepared for anything. Once our bassist's cable fried in the middle of a show. I covered his basslines by playing them with my left hand on my keyboard!

—*Liam O'Neil*, THE STILLS

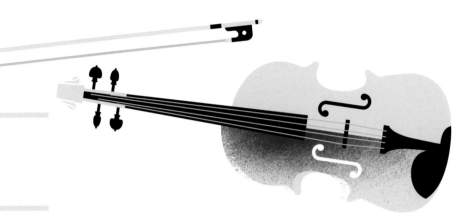

STRINGS
You gotta make it cry

No, you don't call your cello "four-eyes" or beat a violin up before school for its lunch money. String instruments, especially the violin and viola, are just so great at sounding emotional. Think about it: when you're crying watching a movie—whether you're really happy or really sad—you're probably doing it as you listen to strings play in the background. Now that we know the instrument can make us cry, what about making *it* cry?

Take a bow

Guitars (whose strings are picked or plucked) and pianos (whose strings are hammered) can be played quietly or softly, but once a note is played, you can't really change that volume. It just gets quieter until it disappears. But the bow lets you swell a note. This means you can get louder or quieter as you play a single note. This amazing control allows you to connect even more directly to a listener's ear—and their emotions.

Try this: To be heard over drums and guitars, place a pickup near the bridge and use a DI or preamp to capture the sound of your violin.

Fret not

Unlike guitars, the strings are fretless instruments. There are no markings on the necks to tell you where to press to get a certain note. This means that string players can go in between the notes very easily. Now, usually that just means you're playing the wrong note! But in the right piece of music, you can create a sound so sad and lonely, it hits the listener right in the heart.

Expert tip: Try taping down the shoulder rest on your violin if you move around a lot when you play. Otherwise it can collapse and fall off in the middle of a song!

—*Julie Penner,* BROKEN SOCIAL SCENE, DO MAKE SAY THINK, THE WEAKERTHANS

VOCALS
Learn to love what you got

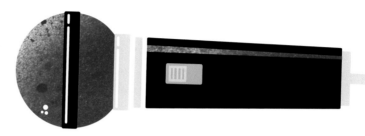

It's the only instrument that comes free with purchase—your own voice! But it's not a gift that you can exchange, so what are those of us born with less-than-perfect voices to do? Some singers have remarkable voices—but if everyone sang like them, how boring would the world be? Some of the most exciting vocals out there are about someone using what little they have to get all that they want.

Listen to singers

From the moment you started speaking, you've been training your voice. You learned language by hearing your parents talk to one another and then imitating that. The same goes for singing. Everyone you hear singing is a teacher—every song a chance to learn something new. When a vocalist really strikes you, listen closely to how they breathe and phrase certain words and try to copy it.

> ***Expert tip:*** Download a vocal warm-up off the Internet. I do four or five steps of one about an hour before I play.
>
> —*Dallas Green,* ALEXISONFIRE

Then listen to your voice

The timbre of your voice is its own unique fingerprint—some are soft and delicate, others are gruff and strong. The key to understanding your voice is your ability to answer these two questions:

What does my voice sound like?—These are the natural characteristics of your voice.

What do I want it to sound like?—These are the things you wish it had.

Once you have that figured out, challenge your voice into making new sounds.

> ***Expert tip:*** If you're nervous or worried about your voice, join a choir. That way you can tuck yourself in among all the other singers, and learn about harmony, too.
>
> —*Feist*

Stay in Key

A SPECIAL MUSICAL INDEX FOR YOU TO USE

On a Final Note: Thanks to all those with whom I've played music over the years, in particular, Scott Remila, Dylan Green, Jarret Kramer, Erik Liddell and the Broken Social Scene family. These people gave good interviews: Melissa Auf der Maur, Buck 65, Ellen Campesinos, Brendan Canning, Joel Carriere, Greg Davis, Jon Drew, Kevin Drew, Leslie Feist, Dallas Green, Emily Haines, Christopher Mills, Liam O'Neil, Julie Penner, Justin Peroff, Ron Sexsmith, Charles Spearin, Louise Upperton, Andrew Whiteman, Rob Zifarelli. Thanks to Jeffrey Remedios, Stephen McGrath, Brendan Bourke, Mandy Ng, and Aron Slipacoff for their help. Valuable editing focus courtesy of Hadley Dyer and Craig Battle. Last but not least, thanks to Carrie Gleason, my intuitive and sympathetic editor; Jeff Kulak, my gifted illustrator/designer; and Mary Beth Leatherdale, who got and kept the ball rolling.